I0022815

Cheryl Clarke, M.S. LMFT | Gregory H. Clarke Sr. M.S. Ed.

THE POWER OF THE 4A's

HOW WE WENT FROM CONTEMPLATING DIVORCE TO A SUCCESSFUL THRIVING MARRIAGE

ISBN: 978-1-943616-47-3

Contents

Legal & Disclaimer

The information contained in this book and its contents is not designed to replace or take the place of any form of medical or professional advice and is not meant to replace the need for independent medical, financial, legal, or other professional advice or services, as may be required. The content and information in this book have been provided for educational and entertainment purposes only.

The content and information contained in this book has been compiled from sources deemed reliable, and it is accurate to the best of the Author's knowledge, information, and belief. However, the Author cannot guarantee its accuracy and validity and cannot be held liable for any errors and/or omissions. Further, changes are periodically made to this book as and when needed. Where appropriate and/or necessary, you must consult a professional (including but not limited to your doctor, attorney, financial advisor, or such other professional advisor) before using any of the suggested remedies, techniques, or information in this book.

Upon using the contents and information contained in this book, you agree to hold harmless the Author from and against any damages, costs, and expenses, including any legal fees potentially resulting from the application of any of the information provided by this book. This disclaimer applies to any loss, damages or injury caused by the use and application, whether directly or indirectly, of any advice or information presented, whether for breach of contract, tort, negligence, personal injury, criminal intent, or under any other cause of action.

You agree to accept all risks of using the information presented in this book. You agree that by continuing to read this book, where appropriate and/or necessary, you shall consult a professional (including but not limited to your doctor, attorney, or financial advisor or such other advisor as needed) before using any of the suggested remedies, techniques, or information in this book.

Text Outline

FOREWORD

Written by Archbishop E. Bernard & Pastor Debra Jordan

The power of the four A's

We are proud to be the pastors of this wonderful couple who we watched come to our church in their teenage years then proceeded to get married and have all of their children in attendance at our church. Gregory and Cheryl are a couple that we have seen weather many ups and downs. In the process of their life, we've watched them transition from a young frustrated couple to a couple that became the best of friends again and are now giving away the precious gift of coupling by sharing both their war stories and victories with others.

Watching them talk about acceptance, appreciation, affection, and agreement; they have found the recipe of what it takes for a marriage to have sustainability. Debra and I have over 40 years in marriage and we are proud to be an example to them of how to create sustainability. This book is more than a couples' book to read; it is also a great work of contemplation concerning relationships. As a power couple, they have created a desired life of their own and have used the extraordinary power of education to bring meaning in the story of their shared experience.

The chapter on understanding appreciation is a powerful takeaway for a marriage. There was a time Cheryl was intense, and Gregory couldn't get a word in. Yet, they both achieved communication levels that have caused them to move light years ahead through the world of agreement.

THE POWER OF THE 4 A'S

Debra and I have read many books on marriage and relationships, as well as many self-help books, however this book surpasses them all. This book has the secret ingredient on how to create and have a successful and prosperous marriage. There aren't many books that can tell you how to have a successful marriage and married couples who can share their own personal experiences on how to do it, especially dealing with the foundational principles of marriage. I believe this book is one of those books that does. It gives the reader all the right ingredients that are necessary to become a power couple. The Bible declares "how can two walk together except they agree." This book teaches how to have a powerful and agreeing connection with your partner.

This book also teaches you how to respect and communicate with clarity, because everyone has their own story. This power truth is applicable to any type of relationship and partnership. This powerful step-by-step book sheds light on how to create a lasting, prosperous and life sustaining marriage This book is a must to anyone and everyone who is contemplating starting a partnership or is currently in one. To have a loving and lasting relationship there must be honesty, and there must be the truth. This book captures the essence of what a valid and working marriage/partnership should look, feel and be like.

As we both read through this book, we can hear the stories that are being told as we see Cheryl and Gregory's life being relived in the people, they are meeting. We tend to discover that we meet no one but ourselves. Everyone we meet or coach is often times ourselves being pressed out in another form. Listening to the stories of the people they have been counseling reminds me of the days they walked through those same pathways of life and found the exit out of the chaos. Congratulations Cheryl and Gregory on finding your authentic voice and being able to give your voice to the world that others may find the incredible power of the four A's in relationship

PREFACE

You can have a successful marriage if you choose!

In our private practice, we focus only on the tools and solutions to implement right now. We seek to provide the greatest impact, because we know firsthand the pain associated with a marriage that has gone terribly wrong. We knew for us and many couples we have worked with that time was of the essence. If these concepts can work for us, they can work for you, as well. The choice is yours. We know your lives are busy, and your results are important to us. We understand many readers may not have the time to go through each and every word in this book. In keeping with this, each section contains an added recap so that readers can quickly access the important points.

There are exercises in the various chapters that will help you get more clarity about where you are currently and where you want to be. It may be tempting to bypass the exercises, but the exercises are a major part of the process shift. We encourage you to do the exercises because understanding concepts intellectually is not enough. Putting into practice what you have learned will ultimately begin to take root.

Part I, is designed to teach couples to learn the concept of **ACCEPTANCE**. In doing so, the 4 A's will help you embrace your partner and also, embrace yourself. Everyone has flaws. However, this book will train you to rename the phrase, *"character flaw" to just "their character."* The renaming of this phrase goes against everything we are taught growing up. Always searching for flaws and imperfections, our minds harp on the negative, making it very difficult to see the positive. This will allow for a more meaningful and fulfilling relationship.

Part II is designed to get underneath and expand your definition of **APPRECIATION**. Creating an atmosphere of appreciation in your relationship is imperative. Couples that display daily appreciation in their relationships continue to evidence overall improvement in their health and wellbeing. Recognizing and understanding this powerful tool of appreciation has limitless value for couples.

Part III delves into the concept of **AFFECTION** and how it differs from intimacy. Affection is a powerful action word that keeps the relationship alive.

Part IV talks about creating a "**Couple's Agreement,**" which is a written document created by the couple and is an honest *"we"* conversation, exploring what the relationship means to both parties individually and as a collective unit.

We are excited to share this valuable information and tools with our readers to help you create the relationship of your dreams.

Note: Some client examples are used for illustrative purposes only. These characters are fictional. Their experiences are similar to clients with whom we have worked with. However, to protect their identity, the characters' names in the examples are fictitious.

INTRODUCTION

Welcome to *The Power of the 4 A's*! These are the tools that will help you enrich and enhance your relationship. A strong, happy, and fulfilling relationship can change your life for the better.

Our Story...

First, we must confess... we were absolutely clueless about marriage many years ago. Neither of us grew up with many good examples of stable, long-lasting marriages. We were both raised in single-parent homes. It's hard to deny that both of our parents' divorces greatly impacted us in a good and bad way. On the good side, we both decided early on that we would stay together no matter what and that divorce was not an option for us. But on the bad side, we had no idea of the complexities that came along with being married, nor did we have a plan in the beginning of how to build a successful marriage that safeguarded us against divorce. We argued and fought a lot. We had no clue how to make our marriage work on our own until we were feeling frustrated, miserable, and contemplating divorce! Yes, divorce! That was probably the lowest point in our lives. But we didn't quit. We decided to FIGHT!

We made the decision to go on an educational journey to learn everything we could about how a successful marriage works. It wasn't long before we realized we had something special. Childhood experiences had given us the resilience to fight and come back even stronger. We embarked upon a new journey and used our own marriage as a living intervention, an intervention which continues to help us on a daily basis achieve a deeper sense of connection, renewed love and communication, and a thriving business.

This book focuses on personal development, education, healing and creating real results that will last a lifetime. This work is based on our own 25+-year marriage and our work with couples over the past ten years. In this vein, we have personally tested all of these ideas, exercises and concepts in our own marriage and concluded what works and what doesn't work. What we have observed through our years of experience with counseling couples and learning from our own marriage is that most couples have the same disagreements. As a result, we have researched and found the tools to help you master your marriage.

THE POWER OF THE 4 A'S

This book covers four distinct aspects of experiencing change in your relationship: 1) Acceptance; 2) Appreciation; 3) Affection; and 4) Agreement. Essentially, we believe there are four key foundational elements for couples to sustain and grow their love. We have an amazing marriage today, and it gets better and better year after year. There is a deeper connection that did not just happen. We have personally used every concept, tool and technique that you will read about in this book, which has yielded lasting results.

The concepts in this book work, but they will only begin to take root when you make a choice to be committed to the process. These concepts can work no matter what has happened in your marriage, whether it's loss of trust, loss of connectedness, infidelity, inability to communicate, lack of appreciation and/or struggles with sex/intimacy. We disagree with the notion, *"There is no such thing as a perfect marriage and a perfect family."* Yes, there is! The perfect marriage and the perfect family are the ones you cultivate together. With the right tools, you can have a happy and fulfilling marriage. Make a choice today to use these essential 4A's to shift your marriage from mediocre to great.

Greg and Cheryl Clarke

www.gregandcherylclarke.com

info@gregandcherylclarke.com

PART I: ACCEPTANCE

"The happiest people in life are able to be themselves. But you cannot be yourself, until you accept yourself."

~ **Jeff Moore**

Chapter 1

THE TRUTH ABOUT ACCEPTANCE

"No amount of self-improvement can make up for any lack of self-acceptance."

~Robert Holden

Acceptance is one of the most important ingredients needed for a successful marriage. However, the truth about accepting oneself for who you are is the prerequisite to be able to accept your relationship, your partner, or anyone, truth be told. Starting with self, speeds up the healing process because you gain personal insight and self-awareness of your behavioral patterns. This Self-Acceptance plays a major role in your decision for a healthy, happy co-existence with your partner.

Self-acceptance is an individual's satisfaction or happiness with oneself and is necessary for good mental health. The more you accept and love yourself, the more stable you will be overall. You must first love yourself before you give love and engage in a relationship. Humans long to be accepted for who and what they are. However, it may be a challenge without fully accepting everything about oneself, such as past traumas, insecurities, upbringing.

Do you really know what type of environment you need to feel accepted in your relationship? This can present a challenge if you do not know how to communicate your needs when you are under stress and your feelings are hurt. This is done first with an understanding of oneself and how to go about doing it. Some couples figure it out by happenstance. However, most people never figure it out without some guidance. Think about the times when you have attempted to tweak, shift or even change something small about yourself. Change can be a struggle, right?

Example

A few years ago, a newly married couple in their early 20's came in for counseling. One of the major issues that came up was the wife perceived her husband's compliments negatively, which constantly sparked an argument between the couple that would escalate. What was really the issue?

After speaking to the wife privately, she expressed exactly what the problem was. She had gained a few extra pounds and felt that her husband was being sarcastic when he commented on her looks. Her husband had no clue that his words were triggering these negative emotions. He was genuinely complimenting her. The problem was the wife felt insecure about her body and somewhat ashamed of the weight that she had gained. She had not fully accepted herself and felt personally attacked when her husband complimented her. It was this insecurity that manifested in the relationship and caused countless fights between the couple.

Do You Accept Yourself as You Are?

As humans, we have a constant drive to change ourselves as we chase our ideal self - an image of who we want to be. A person who does not accept himself/herself, will constantly self-criticize and be the subject of their own internal pressures and unrealistic expectations, which can include second-guessing decision-making, suppressed self-expression and/or a poor self-image. Many couples enter a relationship without answering one simple question for themselves... **Do I accept myself?**

Acceptance is being completely okay with *who* you are and *who* you are not. It starts with the deepest inner parts of self, what you may call your imperfections or flaws. Most of the time, people find it hard to look within, and they find it quite easy to see the flaws of others. In this vein, when you are in a relationship, you are unable to see or hear your partner. In order to hear your partner constructively, you must resolve your own internal conflict accept feedback. Remember, everything begins with YOU. Without accepting yourself, you will not be able to completely accept your partner.

Unconditional Acceptance of Self

In order to accept yourself the way you are, you will need to understand that the goal is not just acceptance, it is the unconditional acceptance of Self. When you choose to accept yourself unconditionally, you begin to love yourself. You will be able to accept your authentic self. This level of acceptance is not a default stage. You are becoming more self-aware. This is needed within the dynamic of a marriage, where you will be constantly challenged by your partner's character traits. Often, people in relationships find it easier to accept "some" parts of themselves but accepting "all" parts is the most challenging.

Couples in partnership must have a healthy sense of self to have a successful relationship. To accept yourself when you did something good is easy (landing your dream job, graduating, achieving your desired weight). However, accepting yourself when you are at your lowest, with all the mistakes and/or regrets, is when you are on the road to accepting yourself unconditionally. People have a tendency to add "*if's*" and/or "*but's*" to acceptance. However, if you do this, you will not be able to fully give yourself to your partner. For example, "*If only I was taller.*" "*But if I had done it sooner...*"

Russell Grieger, a fellow therapist, believes that the unconditional acceptance of Self is the understanding that you are separate from your actions and your qualities. This means recognizing and accepting your mistakes and regrets but refusing to get stuck in those low points and letting them define your overall self.

"Always and unconditionally accept yourself without judgment."
~Russell Grieger

Self-Acceptance and Self-Esteem

"Whereas self-esteem refers specifically to how valuable, or worthwhile, we see ourselves; self-acceptance alludes to a far more global affirmation of self. When we're self-accepting, we're able to embrace all facets of ourselves—not just the positive, more 'esteem-able' parts." ~Seltzer

Self-acceptance is closely related to various other self-concepts, with self-esteem being a close cousin. Self-esteem is how you feel about yourself and whether or not you feel worthy, good, and/or valuable. On the other hand, self-acceptance means acknowledging and accepting that you are who you are.

The research conducted by Berger, E. M. (1952) suggests that self-acceptance has the potential to take our lives and relationships to the next level. Achieving self-acceptance allows us to feel the confidence we need as individuals to co-exist with our partner and others. In the process of recognizing who you are, your strengths, weak points, and everything in between, you will not feel the need to hide from others in shame or self-doubt. Unconditional acceptance of Self lays the groundwork for positive self-esteem. This generally goes hand-in-hand with two different aspects of how we feel and how we think about ourselves.

Acceptance is your ability to recognize your value as a person. In essence, your level of self-worth is defined by feelings of comfortability with self and your abilities. When you do not accept yourself the way you are, you will struggle to reach your full potential in life and/or truly accept others in your life.

Practicing Self-Acceptance

Exploring the process of self-acceptance adjusts the way you react to life's situations. We created an acronym for ACCEPT, which depicts how it helps foster joy and fulfillment within yourself, even when feeling stressed.

A- Activate the Art of Forgiveness

You can only forgive your partner after you learn to forgive yourself. Often, we are left unaware of the guilt, sadness and remorse that we hold over our heads. Confronting these emotions can be very scary. This is why there is an art to forgiveness. You are a masterpiece and one of a kind, so don't rush the process. Take a moment with SELF, and when you feel sad, overwhelmed or unworthy, remove all distractions.

- Sit down.
- Get a journal and begin writing. Allow the feelings to come to the surface. Writing all of it down will give you the room to learn from the past, forgive yourself and only refer to it for feedback to aid you and/or others in the future. In your journaling, note what happened, your feelings and what you learned.
- You can also speak to someone who you deem "safe" and who can handle your emotions and your pain.
- Finally, forgive yourself. Commit to yourself that you will never treat yourself poorly nor live in shame.

This exercise is not about doing things perfectly, but when practiced often enough the feeling of being uncomfortable with self will dissipate. Learning how to forgive yourself can be a transforming opportunity that will aid you in forgiving others. The overall process of forgiveness is a gift to you and your partner.

C- Commit

The next step is a commitment to self, even when no one is around. If you think you can start accepting yourself the way you are in a matter of a few hours, you are wrong. Self-acceptance, especially, unconditional acceptance of Self, is a journey of highs and lows.

There are many successful people throughout history we have either read about or have been told stories about, who have been committed even when it was challenging. Actualizing a healthy sense of self requires perseverance, willingness, courage and faith. Making the conscious decision to commit to this practice will help you gain self-awareness. This is what is needed to effectively communicate who and what you are to others. This process can take months or even years to learn.

It is easy to stay the course when things are good. But when things get challenging, that is when real commitment comes into play. When you have a healthy sense of self you can usually overcome any obstacle, if you are committed to both the health and longevity of the relationship.

- Establish successful habits.
- Celebrate your small wins - they add up to big wins.
- Are you giving as much as you are getting?

C- Communicate with Clarity

All human beings come with a rich history. Everyone has a story. This is what makes us unique. Many couples in our sessions are convinced they are communicating their needs clearly. Oftentimes, the words you say are not being heard the way you meant for them to be heard. Unfortunately, this creates a circular problem that could lead to someone getting hurt. The potential of being hurt comes with the territory of being human. However, you do not have to stay hurt or punish your partner for your past experiences of not being heard.

Misunderstandings in the workplace cause a decrease in productivity, hurt feelings, and unnecessary conflict. Communicating with clarity can eliminate misunderstandings and keep things running smoothly and peacefully. Ensuring clarity in communication is your responsibility. However, if you struggle with self-acceptance, being clear in your own mind could present as a challenge. Here are some ***Tips for Knowing You***:

- Practice your cadence when you speak (watch your tone and speed in conveying your message).
- Become an intentional communicator (be self-aware of harmful words or actions to self and others).
- Finally, make sure the other person hears the message that you sent. Clarity improves connection and engagement because it increases your trust level.

Many of us are afraid of the unfamiliar. People simply stick to those things that they know best. Therefore, when communicating with clarity, start small. It can be uncomfortable at first, but the emotional connection with self and then with your partner will be well worth it. Take a moment to think about what people really mean when they say something to you. Oftentimes, people don't wish to hurt you. They simply do not communicate things as effectively as possible.

Instead of reacting when your partner pushes your buttons, consider using the above techniques when you find yourself getting caught up in unclear communication. One of the biggest struggles in communication for couples is when things seem to get lost in translation. Instead of assuming the worst, take another approach so that you learn to pause and get clarity. Ask what he/she actually means? By pausing to assess what actually occurred, you are able to respond in a more positive, compassionate and conscientious way.

E- Empathy for Your Current and Future Self

One of the biggest truths you need to understand about relationships is that no one in this world judges you as harshly as you judge yourself. Recent research in Harvard Health, it shows that empathy has positive effects on your health, happiness and the pathway to self-acceptance. In general, when we discuss having empathy, it is generally for others, not for oneself. Expressing empathy for your current self and for your future self can be beneficial. Most people have no problem showing empathy or kindness to others. However, one may have a challenge with showing kindness or empathy to themselves. By understanding, you are not be perfect, and that your imperfections are what make you human. Criticizing yourself for everything will keep you stuck or in a holding pattern.

Acceptance requires you to be honest with yourself. Just as you read earlier in the example of the husband's compliment, if you can't be honest with yourself, why should others be honest with you? Accepting your imperfections allows for your growth as a human being! Everyone has an image of their "ideal self" and a list of characteristics your "ideal self" possesses. Let go of who you want to be and embrace all of your "so-called" imperfections. Stop chasing perfection, as you will always be disappointed, and embrace the YOU that YOU are. Doing so will begin to create room for a healthier mindset for acceptance to lay claim in your life.

"There's a crack in everything; that's how the light gets in."

~Leonard Cohen

Allow yourself this opportunity to stop chasing perfection. It will begin to open the door for the acceptance process in your relationship and it will benefit your YOU in the long run. Your choice today to shift will help prepare your future self for a successful life. You get to decide how you will treat this future YOU. Choosing to show empathy to your current and future self not only takes care of you right now, it also takes care of your long-term needs.

P- Positive Thoughts

Your thoughts matter! Becoming more aware of negative thoughts and then learning the techniques to lessen and ultimately eliminate them are key. Positive self-talk and positive thoughts are other ways to increase your acceptance levels. According to the principles of Neuro-Linguistic Programming, through positive self-talk and positive affirmations, you can control your emotional and mental state or status. Positive self-talk is another way to change the way you feel about yourself. Focusing on your strengths and positive qualities will remind you that you are a worthy and valuable human being.

Your Positive Mindset Determines Your Success

Everyone has their strengths and flaws. When we concentrate only on the negatives, we take the positives for granted. Acceptance is a present state of mind. You may be internalizing criticism from someone, which can take you one step further from your quest to achieving self-acceptance and having positive thoughts. At times, we allow others or situations to shift us. Therefore, it is imperative to self-scan to avoid getting stuck there. (We will be covering these strategies later in the book.) Surrounding yourself with positivity and goodness builds a firm foundation to offset the low moments in your life.

Beginning to build this foundation can be as simple as...

- Downloading motivational apps.
- Writing self-affirming notes to yourself.
- Speaking with a supportive friend.

In tough times, when you don't feel secure in yourself or your abilities, turn your attention towards your positive qualities, which is a reminder of your self-worth.

T- Trusting the Process

We have all heard this statement before, *"Just trust the process."* What does it really mean? Trusting has to become your mantra of self-acceptance in implementing the steps to ACCEPT. Understand that you have the potential to hold yourself back when you self-criticize.

- Where is your thinking at this time? BELIEF is one of the strongest attributes, along with FAITH in yourself. However, it must be generated daily. We cannot stress this enough. Every fiber of your being must be in ACTION in order to trust the process.

Take a minute to evaluate your trust level with yourself. Trust will bring you closer to your partner, where you will begin to build a deeper bond with your partner. Trust is the foundation in creating a healthy relationship with your partner and with yourself. Trusting yourself can build your confidence, which makes it easier for you to make decisions and the reduction of your stress level. The good news is, if you do not trust yourself now; with some effort, you can build that trust up over time.

So, how do you build your trust? When you start to feel insecure around others, remind yourself, "It's okay to be me." Once you learn how to better control your thoughts, there is a stronger determination to create the future you desire to have. Giving up on yourself is not an option! You never give up on people that you love. This is something that you must extend to yourself as well, believing in yourself when no one else seems to believe in you, and not letting your failures hold you back. Use your past failures as steppingstones for feedback, pause, and re-evaluation of your plan. Make these a part of your daily practice. If you practice this process over a period of time, you will begin to notice that your reactions and interactions will begin to shift in a more uplifting way.

Couples who struggled in their relationships in the past and who begin to move in a direction of new found acceptance, will initiate to see their partners in a brand-new way and now, handle difficult situations in a more thoughtful way.

Chapter 2

LEARNING TO ACCEPT YOUR PARTNER

For each of us, life brings plenty of challenges. So, why should we bother to suffer needlessly in an empty relationship? It is your life. You get to decide how you want to experience it with the person you have chosen. There are things that can be done to shift the most troubled relationships, but most people simply are not aware of them. You are about to learn what we believe are the best of them.

"Acceptance" is defined by psychologists as a person's assent to the reality of a situation, recognizing a process or condition (often a negative or uncomfortable situation) without attempting to change it or protest it. When a couple first gets together, the relationship is largely, chemically mediated. It's a time when the romance is free-flowing, differences are ignored, and things are good. We most commonly call this the "honeymoon phase" of the relationship.

THE POWER OF THE 4 A'S

In the beginning, you might have viewed marriage as Cheryl did, as some sort of perfect fairytale, where you find the one you love and adore, they support your every dream, and you live happily ever after. Then she got married and there came a reality check really quickly. As time passes, you and your partner should get to know each other even more intimately. Disappointments tend to set into the fabric of the relationship as people in these partnerships create what we call "silent expectations." These expectations have the power to potentially kill relationships.

Successful marriages are built and, just like anything, you need the correct tools. Research has shown that a marriage tends to have a better chance of success when the couple can relate to one another in an interdependent way.

According to Dr. Goldsmith, "interdependent" is when two people, both strong individuals, are involved with each other without sacrificing themselves or compromising their values. They have a balanced relationship. Unfortunately, interdependent couples are not common.

Becoming a couple that lives through interdependency creates a strong foundation for your marriage to grow. It is extremely important to distinguish if you are a co-dependent couple versus an interdependent couple. This can present as a challenge, especially if both parties have not been (or one party has not been) in other healthy relationships before or had a healthy launch into independency from their parents before getting married.

The Interdependent Couple	**The Co-Dependent Couple**
Mutual sense of regard for oneself and each other; balanced.	One person does most of the giving and receives little support or help in return.
Help promotes growth, learning, and self-sufficiency.	Enabling is disguised as help and it creates dependency and stunts personal growth.
Takes responsibility for their own feelings, actions and contributions to the marriage.	Enmeshment or merging of identity and feelings so that neither person functions like a whole, independent person.
Feels free to be your authentic self. A sense of being your own separate, independent person.	Loses sight of your own interests, goals, values and instead, does and says what your partner wants.
Fully experiences your own feelings.	Tends to absorb other people's feelings and suppress your own.
You know you have value even when others are upset with you.	Relies on your partner to make you feel worthy.
Feels safe and secure in your relationship.	Fears rejection, criticism, and abandonment.
Ability to disagree or say "no" without guilt.	Fear of conflict, poor boundaries, and expectation of perfection.
Honesty and the ability to admit mistakes promotes growth.	Denial and defensiveness keep things stagnant. ©Sharon Martin, LCSW

THE POWER OF THE 4 A'S

It is a normal desire to connect with other human beings. A prime example is the craze or normalcy of social media. So, with that said, there is nothing wrong with the desire to connect with others, and to rely on their support. As a couple, you want to cultivate a healthy dependency, better known as interdependency; it shows a healthy mutual balance, where you give and receive, encourage, offer support freely, and so forth. Conversely, with a co-dependent couple, there is usually an imbalance and a lack of regard for the other's individuality, which can often lead to resentfulness, disagreements and blame. Your partner is a unique individual and vice versa.

Acceptance does not mean you are necessarily in total agreement (we will cover agreements later in the book). Instead, it conveys, *"I'm listening and creating a pathway to being heard in the relationship."* When you first get married, you might look up to your partner and view the world through rose-colored glasses. You might love everything about your partner and think that he/she is amazing. Of course, over time, this amazing person starts to appear more and more ordinary. Indeed, the thing that you once loved about your partner may become annoying as time continues to unfold.

One of the major pitfalls married couples encounter over time is the fallacy that their partner needs to change. Now, when it comes to asking your partner to change, do you really think that is a realistic request? In a successful marriage, you must learn how to accept your partner as he/she stands.

Our Example

In our marriage, Cheryl is an extrovert, while Greg is an introvert. Now, this is something that you can't change, as it's the basic personality characteristic! If I tried to be more of an introvert for my husband, I'd be miserable, and if Greg tried to be an extrovert for me, he would be just as uncomfortable and sad. When we go to parties, Cheryl loves to dance, while Greg will do the same old two-step. This created a rift between us, but we had to understand that we are not one and the same. We are two different individuals who have different personalities, likes and dislikes. We had to learn to accept each other for who we are as individuals.

So, instead of being upset with one another about dancing, we agreed before leaving for any party that Greg would dance at least once with Cheryl. That released Greg from the pressure of being on the dance floor with Cheryl for most of the night and freed her to get up and dance as much as she wanted, without feeling mad or sad.

For there to be a wonderful and fulfilling marriage, you have to have self-acceptance and the acceptance of your partner. This is a prime example of a couple working interdependent of each other. If there is a level of undo pressure which can break a marriage and it will become unhealthy for your relationship. Think about it. When you and your partner first got together, things were amazing. The "happy hormones" take over your body and everything about your partner excites you and makes you happy. As time passes, you begin to categorize the characteristics you once found to be interesting or intriguing as flaws, and if you are not careful, you can even drive your partner away.

Acceptance is the key to a healthy relationship. To better understand the concept of acceptance in a relationship, it is important to understand what non-acceptance looks like. We all have our ways of communicating our feelings to our partners that may not be beneficial, which may make them feel like we aren't accepting them. ***To put into simpler words, when you don't accept your partner for who they are, you disrespect and disregard them for who they truly are, what they do, and the life they have chosen for themselves.***

Keep in mind that you can approve of everything about your partner and maybe even agree with them, but not actually accept them. For instance, in your mind, you may have an entirely different expectation of what they should be, act and/or think, feeling that your partner can be doing things that are different or better than what they are currently doing, so they mimic someone you idolize or want them to be. This is what we liken to a "silent expectation," (which we will explain in more detail in the next chapter).

Human beings are social animals. We are socialized into society from childhood and we are constantly told what is and is not acceptable. The process of socialization in itself, is based on the idea of non-acceptance. Breaking the cycle can be difficult, because non-acceptance is actually a social norm in society, as we try to nudge people on what to think and how they should act. However, in order to save your relationship and have a solid marriage, you need to be able to fully accept your partner.

Chapter 3

STEPS TO ACCEPT YOUR PARTNER FOR WHO THEY ARE

Being on the receiving end of non-acceptance can be frustrating and disheartening. It may even drive a wedge between you and your partner and eventually, kill the relationship. After all, no one wants to be around someone who disapproves of their likes, dislikes, hobbies, etc., which is another form of taking each other and the relationship for granted. You may not intend to be non-accepting; however, slowly, over time, it can just happen.

In this chapter, we will be introducing an effective tool called "self-monitoring." This tool was an eye-opener for our marriage. It is an effective tool that STOPS couples from attempting to fix or change each other. It halts the continual cycle of blaming each other, which we see most couples struggling with today. Put the disagreements aside for now. In order for your marriage to be successful, you have to change it. Marriage is 100% all in!

You can begin to accept your partner for who they are by self-monitoring. We have shared simple acts to monitor your behavior that can result in lasting improvements in your marriage.

1. Monitor Your Silent Expectations

Be aware of your silent expectations, which are the thoughts of how you think things should be, and once they are not done you become resentful towards your partner.

Example

A husband and wife, married six years, came in the office for a counseling session. The husband expressed his unhappiness with his wife. He stated, "She doesn't cook anymore, the house is not as tidy, and our sex life sucks!" His wife stated, "Yes, in the beginning I did do a lot of those things. However, we have a 16-month-old son, I work full-time, and I am exhausted."

In this example, we see that this couple's expectations could actually be a little unrealistic in what they could physically do because life had changed. They need a new agreement. (We will show you how to create an agreement later in the book). Ask yourself whether it is something your partner needs to change for you, or if you should change your expectations. Keep in mind that your partner is an individual, and it is not his/her job to live according to your expectations, especially when it is a silent expectation.

2. Monitor the Negative Spin Cycle Thoughts

Negative thoughts can destroy your marriage. You have to take careful steps to ensure that negative thoughts do not disrupt your connection with your partner. Negativity comes in different forms. Sometimes it does not take any effort at all for the automatic insults or criticism to be directed at your partner. Negativity is typically activated by a physical or emotional threat to protect self. When we are faced with obstacles or our needs are not being satisfied, we can go on the defensive. In this vein, going on the attack can activate the default button, the "negative spin cycle," meaning, it becomes second nature to do so. These responses can be deeply damaging, extremely self-serving and can break down the other person to the point they cannot maintain their self-health enough to maintain the relationship.

When a negative thought comes to you about your partner, PAUSE. Remember, negativity shows up as a form of protection. Negativity can easily dominate your thoughts, if you let it. If you fail to recognize the need to reframe negative thoughts, it can lead to triggering that default button that keeps spinning over and over, like a washing machine stuck on the spin cycle, and never stop.

Here are examples of a negative spin cycle:

- *You never do anything for me.*
- *You never want to spend time with me anymore.*
- *You are always complaining.*

Train yourself to refrain from using the words "always" and "never." Reframe your thought with a positive response. This will take practice! Instead of viewing your partner in negative ways, begin to train your mind to PAUSE and replace those negative thoughts with positive thoughts, what you love about your partner, and then respond. Remember, marriage is for a lifetime. Some have referred to marriage as a marathon not a sprint. Any efforts you make to move away from negativity will greatly benefit your marriage.

3. Monitor Living in the Present

In some cases, you may not accept your partner because you are dwelling on painful memories of the past. You might have a tendency to compare your partner or the things he/she does to the events of the past, which can harmfully impact your relationship over time. Understanding the pathways to accepting your partner, means shifting your present view of them. Sure, we all make mistakes. However, holding onto those mistakes as evidence to prove a point, does not allow the relationship or your partner room to grow from their mistakes.

There is so much power in refusing to bring up your partner's past mistakes to disprove of something they do in the moment. Don't hold things against them when they have tried to change and grow. The key is learning how to control your reaction, only referencing the past for feedback, never for blame. When done correctly, the couple will begin to resolve problems more effectively. We all can be and will be triggered to bring up the past. However, bringing up the past can interrupt the healing process. If you are triggered...

- First, identify the trigger (person, place, situation)
- Second, identify your mood or attitude shift (anger, sadness, frustration, etc.)
- Third, identify your automatic thought. Acknowledge the thought. Do not attempt to suppress it.
- Fourth, after you have identified the above, begin to actively shift the thought to now. (Think about your visualizing hope exercise. Often, the pressures we put on our partners are a direct result of our personal criticisms. Once you stop judging yourself, you have made a critical step in accepting your partner. Living in the past will always hold you back from

accepting your partner for who he/she is, which can ultimately, damage the marriage. Monitoring your present results in hope for the future.

4. Monitor How You Are Showing Empathy

Put yourself in your partner's shoes. Feeling hurt, neglected? How do you like to be treated? Oftentimes, when couples are having a disagreement, it is natural to wish to be heard. However, interjecting empathy, thinking of what they need in that moment exhibits true care for one another. When done by both parties, it can provide a space for the couple to fully express themselves without judgment. When you show your partner empathy, it demonstrates acknowledgment of the acceptance that you would like in return. Remember, extending empathy all goes hand-in-hand. When a couple is mindful to pause and show empathy, they create a safe space within their relationship for both parties to be truly accepted and heard. This will take some time. In the beginning, however, it is vital to remember to stick with the process. Love is patient, and love is kind.

Part II: Appreciation

"A moment of gratitude makes a difference in your attitude."

~Bruce Wilkinson

Chapter 4

UNDERSTANDING APPRECIATION

As a marriage progresses naturally, it is not uncommon to take some things for granted. In fact, this happens in every relationship. In one way or another, there will be a point in every relationship where there will be one partner or both complaining about not feeling appreciated by their partner. It's natural, but it's not healthy.

Appreciation is a powerful tool. When a couple intentionally practices appreciation, they create new value with deliberate actions that will enrich their journey together for a lifetime. They always look for the good in each other. Appreciation may be one of the most overlooked of all the A's by couples on a daily basis. Cultivating appreciation does not cost any money and it does not take much time, but there are massive rewards.

Think about it. You spend eight to ten hours at work per day. How much does your manager, co-workers or customers appreciate you for what you have done or are doing? Then you go home and possibly receive the same treatment or worse from your partner. Studies have shown that the lack of appreciation affects individuals in an adverse way. Statistics have shown that because you live with your partner, share your life and your ups and downs with them, their opinion matters to you probably more than your co-workers, which can affect your overall well-being.

A lack of appreciation in your marriage can affect your health as well. Studies have revealed that couples who show daily appreciation in their relationship report overall improvement in their physical and mental health. A 2012 study revealed that people who show appreciation or feel appreciated report feeling healthier than other people. They take better care of themselves, exercise more often and are more likely to attend regular check-ups with their doctors, which is likely to contribute to further longevity.

Appreciation also improves your mental health. It decreases the potential of a slew of damaging emotions ranging from bitterness, animosity, frustration, worry and doubt that can infiltrate your marriage. For a healthy marriage, it is important to recognize that both parties are valuable to the unit and when it is done effectively; the overall happiness will increase in a positive way.

Example

A couple came to us for marriage counseling. The wife was a stay-at-home mother of two, and the husband worked as an investment banker and earned a six-figure salary. Their marriage was going through a rough patch because the wife didn't feel appreciated. "I work all day to impress my husband. I clean, I feed the kids, take care of them, take them to school and after-school activities, come home and cook a meal for my husband. But I still don't get so much so as a thank you! Then I do it all over again the next day!" The husband, on the other hand, had no idea what was wrong. "I work hard all day and come home to a nagging, upset wife, when all I want is to unwind."

In this case, both the husband and wife were feeling unappreciated, resulting in the quality of life within their marriage was deteriorating. You and your partner are individuals within the relationship, and while you do divide responsibilities in the life that you have created together; you do not owe each other for the things you do. In other words, it is important to acknowledge and appreciate your partner for the things he/she does for you and vice versa, whether it is making breakfast in the mornings, taking out the trash or filling up the car with gas. All the gestures your partner does for you and your family are to be appreciated so that your partner can feel validated, which leads to a healthy marriage.

THE POWER OF THE 4 A'S

As we mentioned earlier in this book, it is easier to look at the negatives of a person and a relationship. However, when someone in the relationship does not feel appreciated, it leads to animosity, which can potentially lead to separation, if you're not careful. Men and women process appreciation in completely different ways. We all have heard the phrase, *"Men are from Mars, women are from Venus,"* and that is a good thing. But it means that the way we relate to each other can present a challenge in how we appreciate each other, because expressing your appreciation makes you vulnerable. Over time, after expressing your appreciation to your partner, a deeper emotional connection can form, which is an important factor of truly happy couples.

Expressing your appreciation to your partner is imperative for a healthy, thriving relationship and boosts your partner's sense of acceptance. When your partner does not feel appreciated, his/her quality of life in the relationship decreases and they feel like they are being taken for granted. It can be as simple as saying, "Thank you." Showing appreciation can improve the quality of your marriage.

Appreciation is something we long for from our childhood years. We crave appreciation! Think about when you were in grade school, you worked harder in class once you were appreciated by your teacher. You thrived in a sport when your coach or parents acknowledged how good you were. In fact, you learned basic skills in your life through appreciation, because appreciation is a positive reinforcement. When each partner feels appreciated, both parties are more likely to be present in the relationship.

Example

A newly married couple came to us for counseling. Their problem was miscommunication and the increased fighting between them. Whenever the husband commented on something about his wife, she became upset. "He always tells me how useless I am and how I can't do anything right." Exploring deeper, we discovered the real issue. The husband was extremely vocal about the things he thought were negative about his wife and the things she did not do or did not do right. However, he rarely appreciated his wife for the things she did right.

The problem was the husband appreciated his wife, but he only expressed it to his friends and family. He would tell others how wonderful a person she was, how she made him feel, and what an amazing cook, mom and overall home manager she was, but he never expressed those things directly to his wife. Consequently, the wife felt that her husband had a negative mindset concerning her and did not like or appreciate her (which wasn't the case), so she started to respond to him in that manner.

Take time out of your day to appreciate your partner for his/her contributions in meeting your together goals. Their actions and efforts should not be taken for granted because while you may feel secure in your marriage, chances are your partner may be feeling the opposite. In the above example, the problem was not that the husband did not appreciate his wife. In fact, he thought the world of his wife and talked highly of her to others whenever he had the opportunity. However, the most important person did not hear the things he said and was left feeling unloved and unappreciated.

Appreciate and love your partner and tell them how you feel on a daily basis. Every relationship and every marriage are unique in its own way. But one thing that is universal in all relationships and marriages; you must communicate with each other in order to connect on a deeper level. After all, how else can you communicate your needs and desires to your partner? Learning to be kind and appreciative of your partner is of vital importance.

There is something called "stranger kindness," which is the tendency to be more polite and nice to someone you don't know. This is seen as being a socially acceptable exercise. You may know of it as "good manners." However, that courtesy is often not extended as you start getting closer and more comfortable with the person. In your comfort zone, you often stop using words like, "thank you," "please," etc.

If you desire a happy, thriving marriage, both parties must make it their business to intentionally appreciate each other.

Never Assume

Let your partner know that you are fully aware of how and what he/she is contributing to the marriage and to you. Do not make assumptions. If you feel you are not being appreciated, let your partner know.

Example

A client once shared a story: "My husband and I were sleeping in our bed on a chilly winter night. When I woke up that night to go to the bathroom, I saw that my husband was covered in the blanket, while I was not, and for some reason I felt hurt. I always make it a point to put the blanket on my husband in the winter if I come to bed after he does, but I am sad that he doesn't do the same for me."

While this case is not directly related to appreciation, it is related to assumption. The wife simply assumed that her husband was not being considerate of her feeling cold, although she was genuinely cold. But her assumption that she was not important to him was unfair. It is unfair to assume that because you are in a relationship with someone, he/she is a "mind reader," no matter how long you have been together. Your partner will only know what you are thinking when you communicate your thoughts. In the end, the husband simply thought that his wife wasn't feeling as cold when he went to bed, because the prior few nights she expressed how warm she was feeling. Essentially, he thought he was being considerate.

Be considerate of your partner's feelings and always ask. Do not assume you know! Each person in the relationship brings his/her own unique set of opinions and ideas. It is important to know for sure by communicating your thoughts verbally. For example, if you are watching a movie on the couch and you feel thirsty, on your way to the kitchen simply ask your partner, "*I'm going to the kitchen, would you like anything?*" If you see your partner working on the computer, before you start a conversation with him/her, ask, *"Honey, do you have a minute?"* Then wait for him/her to respond. Something as simple as asking your partner questions can drastically improve the quality of your relationship, because questions bring you to an inquiry stance, which makes your partner feel that you are considering them, even in the smallest gestures.

Learning to apologize and saying, "I'm sorry" if your partner feels hurt or wronged by either your actions or your words, is also a way of displaying appreciation in the relationship. Choose to put hurt behind you, reframing your negative thoughts and feelings with positive feelings of love, where both parties grow from the event. It is also very important to consider each other as the ultimate teammates in love, spiritual support, and as financial partners. While the two of you are individuals, what one does affects the other. Therefore, keep in mind that every choice you make will affect your partner someway, somehow. Consider your partner in all your decisions.

Example

A couple came in for a session. The husband shared his issue with a decision that his wife made about changing her working hours without discussing it with him. The wife decided that she would change her work hours from the traditional, 9:00 AM - 5:00 PM, to 11:00 AM - 7:00 PM. She didn't consider her partner or factor in his opinion while making the decision. She stated that she didn't realize how big of an effect the simple change in schedule would have on their marriage. This is because their time together at home was cut short! Before the shift change, the couple went to work and created quality time in the evening. They had created a ritual - come home and unwind, cook, watch their favorite TV show, etc. However, because of the change in schedule, the responsibilities of the couple changed and they couldn't spend any quality time with each other.

It is essential to consider your partner. It is very important to include, not exclude your partner. Remember, you are a team.

Chapter 5

IMPLEMENTING APPRECIATION IN YOUR RELATIONSHIP

In a marriage, it is all too easy to get caught up in the daily grind of life and forget how essential your partner is in preserving or building a successful marriage. Through appreciation, couples can begin to communicate their value. By implementing behaviors that display appreciation in the relationship on a daily basis, couples will look for more opportunities to value each other. The marriage unit is a valuable entity. However, when appreciation is not present in the relationship, the connection depreciates and has the potential to unravel.

The addition of appreciative behaviors in a marriage can radically alter how one functions within a relationship. In fact, when your partner feels appreciated; they value the relationship more. It is no longer a struggle to show love. In fact, it becomes the common language within the relationship. Without question, the relationship will grow new roots, strengthening the bond for many years to come. When done correctly, a couple will notice that appreciation within the relationship reduces, 1) the number of arguments; 2) the potential for extramarital affairs; and 3) overall unhappiness.

We want you to consider the fact that embarking on a life with more appreciative behaviors, when practiced enough, will eventually stick. Implementing the first "A" (Acceptance) discussed in the beginning of this book, coupled with the understanding that aspects of the relationship are likely to change over time, couples will find it easier to appreciate each other.

In this section of the book, we will share five ways you can begin to implement behaviors of appreciation toward your partner. Consistency in displaying behaviors of appreciation over time, could lead to a new conditioning of the brain that can have lasting benefits for the overall relationship.

1. Saying Thank You

You may be asking yourself, are we doing an entire exercise on thanking our partner? Well, yes, because it is the simplest way to appreciate each other. Saying thank you for the small things can go a long way. It allows you to fully acknowledge your partner for what he/she has said or done.

<u>**Example**</u>:
"You look great tonight."

Wrong Response: *"Yeah right, you're just saying that? I think I look fat."*

Right Response: *"Thank you. I'm glad you think so."*

Yes, your partner may say or do things genuinely out of love, but not fully accepting their comments of appreciation can lessen the chances of your partner giving you another compliment and/or gesture of appreciation. Receiving and giving comments of appreciation, such as "thank you," should be an enjoyable experience. Do not sabotage the appreciation process. Enjoy accepting, giving and receiving.

2. **Be Self-Aware**

Cultivating a sense of self-awareness benefits the overall relationship. Becoming self-aware is possible once you cultivate self-acceptance and develop a deeper appreciation of self. Practice is the key and can be well worth the effort. Highlighting qualities and attributes of your partner that you can appreciate is vital. Ask yourself the question - has my partner stopped appreciating me? Have I stopped appreciating my partner?

One of the major reasons couples refrain from showing appreciation to one another is they themselves do not feel appreciated. When you appreciate your partner, it paves the way and makes it easier for your partner to appreciate you. Many couples find appreciation useful. However, it is not commonly practiced on a consistent basis.

Example

Elena and Josh had been married for 22 years and were facing a problem. Josh felt that Elena didn't appreciate him anymore and had started taking him for granted. She didn't thank him for washing the dishes every night after dinner nor surprising her with flowers, just because. However, it turned out that Elena felt the same way about Josh - not thanking her for making dinner or dropping him off at the train every morning. They both were unaware of the roles they played in withholding appreciation when they felt unappreciated. So, the vicious cycle continued until they learned and implemented the tools of the 4 A's.

Self-awareness of your role keeps you present to actively practicing being appreciative of your partner.

3. Watch Your Tone

We talked about reinforcement and consistency earlier in this section and how these concepts work in relationships in regards to appreciation. We have all heard the saying, *"It's not what you say—it's how you say it!"* It is very important to be mindful of your tone when speaking to your partner.

In the book, *The Relationship Cure*, Dr. Gottman teaches, in communication, only seven percent of meaning comes from the spoken word, while thirty-eight percent comes from tone of voice and speech patterns. Words that may seem neutral can be spoken with a sarcastic or demeaning tone of voice, causing the listener to feel hurt and disrespected. Your words matter, but the tone in which you speak those words communicates even more than the words themselves. Your tone of voice has a direct correlation to long-term success in your marriage. Learning to use this dynamic tool effectively in your marriage will enhance your relationship and cause you and your partner to feel special in the relationship.

Example

The next time you or your partner become upset or frustrated with each other, manage your emotions. Pause and ask yourself, "What is my emotional state right now?" Pay attention to what your inner voice is saying before you say it. Chances are you probably need to be mindful of your tone of voice, especially when emotions are high. Practice catching yourself before you speak and offer the same words in a more kind and loving way. This one simple mindset shift can profoundly change your relationship for life.

Adopting a respectful and loving tone shows your partner that you appreciate, care and love them and never want to be hurtful or disrespectful. Once you are aware of what you are feeling, you can better manage your emotions, your tone and words more effectively.

4. Create More Opportunities to Show Appreciation

If you are like most couples or people in general, your workday is filled with tasks, deadlines and priorities. You can easily miss an opportunity to extend appreciation. Remind yourself to stop and show appreciation throughout the day. The real value lies in being able to display your appreciation on a consistent basis. Considering the following scenarios as you create opportunities to show your partner appreciation, will prove this tool to be very powerful when used correctly. Implementing these opportunities will not only show your partner that you recognize what they are doing, but also what they have done. Oftentimes, it is the simple things that yield the big results.

Example

The next time you and your partner are apart, send a "middle of the day" text - "I'm just sitting here at my desk thinking about you. I can't wait to see your face." A text like this sends a very clear message, "I don't take you for granted. I'm thinking about you. I appreciate you."

In relationships and marriages, it is easy to feel that your partner doesn't appreciate or love you the way you love them. You need to create those opportunities to show appreciation in the morning, during the day, in the evening, on the weekends. These moments can even happen when you are apart. They do not have to take up much time, but you do have to be intentional and deliberate.

5. Give A "Just Because Gift"

When was the last time you gave your partner a gift just because, not because it was their birthday, a holiday or an anniversary? If I had to guess, your answer would be, "Not very often." Developing the "giving" trait is essential for establishing meaningful relationships. As humans we are conditioned to focus on what we are not getting, instead of what we are not giving. As you begin to focus on giving to your partner, it will cause your relationship to grow and a greater sense of compassion and love.

As both parties collaboratively implement "giving" they will develop a deeper understanding of each other's needs. I know you have heard the old saying, "Actions speak louder than words." Your partner will remember how you made him/her feel. Letting your partner know that he/she is appreciated, creates a sense of security in your marriage and helps build a solid foundation. As a result, you will strengthen your bond and build trust. Your willingness to show your appreciation for your partner is well worth the effort.

A small gift can brighten their day. It doesn't always have to be a physical gift, like a box of chocolates, or something big or expensive. It is the thought that counts. When you let your partner know that you appreciate them, you also make them feel loved and respected at the same time.

<u>Example</u>

- **Surprise your partner with flowers or chocolates.**
- **Surprise your partner by taking them out to lunch or dinner.**
- **A handwritten love letter doesn't cost a thing.**

When you let your partner know that you appreciate the things they do for you, they begin to feel reassured about your love for them. If your partner gives you a gift, thank him/her. Maybe it will inspire you to reciprocate in kind. Now, with this being said, if one or both of you are highly competitive individuals, remember, it is not a competition. It is a space to create a new habit, a loving, giving, intimate relationship with your partner.

To cultivate a lasting, committed relationship, both parties must participate in nurturing each other's feelings. You should feel good as the "giver" and want to give again. Start re-energizing your relationship today with implementing at least or more of these appreciation tools shared in this chapter.

Chapter 6

UNDERSTANDING THE SIGNIFICANCE OF APPRECIATION

We can use our appreciation consciously and intentionally to transform our relationship and cultivate a space to grow together. We've gone through the importance of appreciation in a marriage in the previous chapters, but we rarely think about the "why" or the "significance" of appreciating our partners. Living intentionally and interjecting healthier habits will begin to align a couple with a deeper sense of "connect-ability," which takes the marriage to the next level.

When your partner feels appreciated, it often leads to transformation within the relationship. It appears that while we all seem to know that we like being appreciated, we tend to forget how significant expressing appreciation is to our partner. The good news is both feeling and learning the skill of appreciation can strengthen the bond between you and your partner. Learning how to be a more appreciative couple begins to positively transform every area of your life, family, community and society. Becoming more mindful of demonstrating appreciation for your partner creates a loop of appreciation that can develop not just for your partner, but for yourself, as well.

In this section of the book, we will share five shifts within the relationship that are the result of appreciation. Each of these shifts occurs when partners engage in appreciative behaviors within the context of the relationship. These behaviors will significantly benefit the marriage.

1. Appreciation shifts your outlook. Is your cup half empty or half full? Your answer to this question says a lot about your outlook. The reason so many couples struggle is that naturally, we often do not look for reasons to give appreciation or be appreciative either in our relationships or at our place of business. As humans, we are self-absorbed most of the time. We are focused on how we feel.

- Did you know that staying in an appreciative state of mind can absolutely change your outlook?
- Did you know that how you start your day can predict how the rest of your day can go?

Your mornings are important. Upon waking up, be intentionally fortified with a positive outlook. Implementing some type of spiritual practice into your daily morning routine, like praying, yoga or meditation can aid you in conditioning your mind, emotions and overall outlook.

2. Appreciation shifts your mood. Your moods can be contagious. They can have a major cause and effect on others around you. Many people are unaware of how significantly their mood changes can impact their relationship with their partner.

Example

Your wife says a nasty comment and you give a nasty comment right back to her. Why? We tend to get caught up in negative moods. Matching your partner's negative mood can only trigger an increase in negativity. In your relationship, it is imperative that you take responsibility for your actions and mood. The next time your partner is in a bad mood, refuse to engage. Choose to take a walk, take deep breaths, or pause before responding. This is a great way to display how appreciative you are of your relationship and keep the marriage on a healthy track.

3. Appreciation shifts your respect and trust levels. Couples who are intentional about showing their appreciation to their partners will find that their respect and trust levels are higher. When your partner expresses his/her thoughts or ideas, do you take them seriously? Do you communicate clearly? Communication is a major part of appreciating one another, which leads to building respect and trust. Couples should feel comfortable sharing their thoughts without fear of judgment. Shared respect for one another results in greater inner peace and joy.

When a couple respects and fully trusts one another in their marriage, it means they understand that their partner is a valuable individual and they learn to co-exist with their uniqueness. Trust is important on the individual level and as a collective unit. Respect and trust work hand-in-hand in a relationship. Therefore, it is essential for a marriage to have both respect and trust to be successful. Respecting your partner's individuality welcomes that same respect in return.

4. Appreciation shifts the couple to building a stronger bond. As you continue to appreciate your partner, you will notice a significantly stronger bond begin to form. You will find that you cannot wait to get home to see your partner, instead of opting to stay late at the office. You will even opt to hang out with your friends less days out of the week. When you feel appreciated you want to stay longer in the relationship, which leads to increased happiness, long-lasting marriages, an inviting environment and overall well-being.

You may be asking, in what ways can our bond grow? You and your partner may feel a sense of freedom to be who you are and be transparent in your conversations. Even conversations that were considered tough in the past, have a tendency to become easier. Implementing thoughts of love on a daily basis will build a much stronger and more genuine relationship.

Example

A couple came in for counseling. They reported feeling fed up. They felt they tried everything. We gave them the appreciation challenge. They had nothing to lose so they tried it. They discovered how to speak to one another once again and built a stronger bond, which prepared them during a storm or rough patch.

5. **Appreciation shifts the entire trajectory.** Research indicates showing appreciation makes couples feel happier about self, but it has been shown to lead to more commitment within the overall relationship and future endeavors. (Personal Relationships, 22 (2015), 536–549.)

THE POWER OF THE 4 A'S

Couples experiencing long-term success have learned the amazing skill of focusing on the positive. This must become a daily practice, where couples are intentionally expressing appreciative thoughts to their partners. In choosing to do this, couples will slowly shift the trajectory of their relationship to a more positive place. Doing and saying the "same old thing," is not going to yield new results. The "same old thing" will result in you having an average, ordinary marriage, and it doesn't shift you onto the new path of an amazing, extraordinary marriage.

When appreciation is present in a marriage, the couple can grow *together*. However, there is no guarantee. It merely gives you a higher probability of having a successful future. Appreciation is an essential ingredient in your marriage if you want it to last forever. As time passes, people get comfortable with their partners. As the relationship evolves, each party assumes different roles and may stop showing each other appreciation, which can have a catastrophic effect on your relationship. Your partner cannot read your mind. The only way your partner is going know how you feel about them, is by your words and actions. If your partner feels unappreciated, they will probably withhold appreciation. This could cause major problems within your relationship and can lead to misunderstandings, which can all be avoided by consistently showing appreciation to your significant other.

Part II - Chapter Highlights at A Glance: Appreciation

Psychologists define appreciation as the recognition and enjoyment of the good qualities of someone or something.

- For a healthy marriage, it is important to recognize that you both are valuable to the unit.
- It is easier to focus on the negatives in a person and a relationship because sometimes the negatives are more obvious than the positives, thus you concentrate more on them. As a result, you create a negative mindset towards your partner, which can change the way you think about him/her.
- When your partner does not feel appreciated, his/her quality of life in the relationship decreases and they feel like they are taken for granted.
- In a marriage, value is essential. It helps both parties understand where they stand in each other's life and what they mean to each other. It is through appreciation that you let your partner know their value in your life.
- When you start to show your partner that you appreciate them and what they do for you, you eliminate a lot of issues that can arise between the two of you.

Implementing appreciation in your relationship:

- **Say Thank You:** Saying "thank you" fully acknowledges your partner for what they have said or done.
- **Be Self-Aware:** Having a sense of self-awareness of what your role is keeps you present to actively practicing being appreciative of your partner.
- **Watch Your Tone:** Your tone of voice is directly correlated to the long-term success of your marriage. Learning to use this dynamic tool of controlling your tone of voice effectively when speaking to each other is key, and the more special you and your partner will feel in the relationship.
- **Create More Opportunities to Show Appreciation:** Couples need to create opportunities to show appreciation in the morning, during the day, in the evening and/or on the weekends. These opportunities can even happen when you are apart. None of them take much time, but you have to intentionally create the opportunities more often to show appreciation.
- **Give a "Just Because" Gift:** A small gift can brighten your partner's day. It doesn't have to be big and expensive. It's the thought that counts. When you let your partner know that you appreciate him/her, you also make them feel loved and respected at the same time.

Understand the "why" or the "significance" of appreciating your partner more. There are five shifts in which showing appreciation to your partner can significantly benefit the relationship.

- **It shifts your outlook.** Many people are simply too self-absorbed. They are focused on how they feel and immediate interests. But when you change your outlook, you intentionally begin to acknowledge just how great your partner really is.
- **It shifts your mood.** Your moods can be contagious and will have a major cause and effect on others around you. Oftentimes, we are unaware of how significantly bad or good an impact our mood can have our partner.
- **It shifts your respect and trust levels.** Couples who are intentional about showing their partner appreciation will find that their respect and trust levels are higher. To respect and trust fully in a marriage means understanding that your partner is a valuable individual and learning how to co-exist with their uniqueness. Trusting each other and helping each other grow as individuals and as a collective unit is essential to a healthy relationship.
- **It shifts your bond.** When you feel appreciated you want to stay longer in the relationship. In fact, there is a big

correlation, which leads to increased happiness, long-lasting marriages, an inviting environment, and overall well-being.

- **It shifts the entire trajectory.** Making the decision to implement appreciation within the relationship can slowly shift the entire trajectory of the relationship in a positive way. Doing and saying the "same old thing" isn't going to yield new results. The "same old thing" will yield an average, ordinary marriage and it doesn't shift you on a new path of having an amazing, extraordinary marriage.

Part III: Affection

"Love is not to be purchased, and affection has no price."

~ St. Jerome Emiliani

Chapter 7

UNDERSTANDING THE IMPORTANCE OF AFFECTION

When conceptualizing a healthy marriage, oftentimes, people only think of love, commitment, and good communication skills - all necessary in every relationship. However, we rarely think about our behaviors within the context of the relationship and the roles we both play to obtain a long-lasting, loving, healthy successful marriage.

Let's start with some definitions. According to Dictionary.com, "affection" is defined as a gentle feeling of fondness and liking. "Intimacy" is defined as showing a close union; or a combination of particles or elements; an intimate mixture. When you are affectionate towards your partner, there exists feelings of being deeply cared for that begin to cultivate intimacy within the relationship, and the couple begins to join their hearts to one another. The lack of affection in a marriage might be an indication that the couple is struggling with intimacy. Couples should be committed to making affection a healthy practice – not in clingy, needy or demanding ways, but in positive, healthy ways, which we will discuss in more detail later in this book.

Let's evaluate affection from a biological/neuroscience research point of view. Affection in a relationship works by rewiring the brain in the direction where love actually becomes a healing force according to Deepak Chopra's point of view in his book, "The Path to Love". A simple act of affection influences your partner's hormones, which goes as deep as aiding in cell repair and even promoting homeostasis, a biological self-regulation and self-repair mechanism.

Theoretically, intimacy and affection seem to go hand-in-hand. Couples in long-term relationships may struggle over time if there is a lack of displaying levels of affection.

Let us talk about our personal history in our marriage. When my husband and I were at the lowest point in our marriage, affection and intimacy had become nonexistent within our relationship. We were failing to display our love through affection. You may not know how, why or when this will happen. The affection just diminish we didn't have the tools to help foster affection.

We have found couples that experience a lack of intimacy and displays of affection, oftentimes find it has become an issue for one or both for numerous reasons, such as stress, finances, children or overall concern about the future. The truth is we cannot control everything that happens to us. Affection is a powerful ACTION word.

You can tell your partner you love him/her. However, demonstrating your love through kisses, hugs, rubs, I love you texts and calls, etc., is more powerful, because it will cause your partner to feel loved, cared for and special. In other words, finding ways to show affection to your partner feeds the relationship and the soul of your partner. If being intimate involves the joining of your souls and the sharing of your hearts, it is imperative for the couple to have the first "A" (Acceptance) of self-mastery.

Affection is a vital ingredient in your relationship. It requires both parties to define what affection and intimacy look like to each of them individually. When one partner is affectionate toward the other, the following messages are sent:

1. You are important to me. I will care for you and protect you.
2. I am concerned about the problems you face and will be there for you when you need me.

A simple hug can say those things. There are many other ways to show our affection - a greeting card, an "I love you" note, a bouquet of flowers, holding hands, walks after dinner, back rubs, phone calls, conversations with thoughtful and loving expressions of love. All these suggestions effectively communicate affection. Affection is essential in a relationship. Without it many people feel totally alienated within their relationships. Affection causes both parties to become emotionally bonded and experience a sense of safety in the relationship.

If your partner does not show affection, you may feel alone or feel like you are not enough. It is normal to feel the need for affection. Abraham Maslow, is a well-studied psychologist whose focus was on human needs and it is no surprise that affection is found to be very important. Level 3 of Maslow's hierarchy of needs is love and belonging needs, where once the physical survival and safety needs are being regularly met, a need for love, affection and belonging begin to emerge. Level 3 needs result from the fact that human beings are sociable and need relationship with others.

Did you know that the lack of affection is one of the top reasons couples seek therapy? Is your partner the first person you think to go to in order to share your wins or when you need comfort or support?

Research conducted by Horan and Booth-Butterfield found that affection is somewhat of a thermometer that allows couples to gauge their intimacy levels, a major piece of the puzzle that holds couples together, especially through tough times. When you affectionately communicate with your partner, you are investing and building in a relationship that can stand the test of time. Studies have also found that your level of satisfaction and commitment is directly related to the amount of affection that you receive from and express to your partner. They also suggested that over a 15-year period, satisfaction and commitment are important predictors of relational persistence.

Together, the above findings suggest that affection is important in both good and troubled times. Expressing and receiving affection in a marriage comes with loads of benefits.

Example

Beth and Robert came in for a counseling session. Beth is a stay-at-home mom and Robert runs his business. At the time, they had been married for 30 years, but their relationship was not in a good place. The issue was that Beth was trying hard to connect with her husband by talking to him and showing him affection through hugging and cuddling. But Robert never reciprocated the affection. On top of that, he "pushed" her away (figuratively) whenever she tried to cuddle him. His excuses for doing so were always good and included reasons like:

- *He just got home from work and needed his space or "me time."*
- *He gets too hot when they cuddle for long periods of time.*
- *He is too exhausted and just wants to go to bed.*

Beth would even suggest that they cuddle until he falls asleep, but he would roll his eyes at her and spend a good amount of time scrolling through emails on the phone before bed. While Robert was honestly satisfied with his relationship, Beth was not satisfied. She tried to communicate her feelings to him, but he would dismiss her feelings and say, "How can you be mad about that AGAIN?" What may be insignificant for Robert was a big issue for his wife. Beth's quality of life and her happiness in the marriage kept declining and she feared that she needed to embrace this chapter of life.

In this case, Beth wanted to bring back the affection in her marriage. Robert was very much in love with his wife, but he did not show it. If your partner does not *feel* loved, then they are not going to be happy or satisfied with the relationship. All Beth wanted was her husband's love and affection.

Dismissing your partner's feelings is hurtful. If one of you is hurting or affected by something, it will affect the relationship in a negative way. If you hurt your partner, then at some point, you will also get hurt. Expressing your affection sends a powerful message to your partner through your words, physical touch and other actions. Let them know that you deeply care and love them. A loving touch, in particular, is vital to the overall happiness and elevation of the relationship. It can create that connection and fulfillment for which you both long.

Chapter 8

DISTINGUISHING A HEALTHY, AFFECTIONATE/INTIMATE MARRIAGE

Affection is normal and is an essential "A" that a marriage needs to be successful. Oftentimes, it can be hard to distinguish between affection, intimacy, sex and other related things. So, now that you know what affection is, you should also know what it is not. Showing affection to your partner feeds the overall wellness of the mind, body and soul of the relationship. However, if we look to our partner to fulfill our overall needs for happiness and love, then we may be left feeling disappointed and/or rejected.

Remember, your partner is not responsible for your happiness. Rather they should know what makes you happy or brings you joy. We can create unhealthy expectations. If you fail to learn how to effectively distinguish and then communicate in a clear and effective manner, then you may not get the results you desire.

Your marriage requires affection, physical touch and verbal gestures from each partner. However, it is important to understand how your partner receives and gives affection. This provides for a better understanding of how to effectively convey affection in your relationship. You must take into account each other's upbringing and your understanding of what constitutes affection. Just think, you or your partner may continuously become annoyed when confusing an invitation to spoon with having sex. One may even find themselves becoming upset with their partner, and the truth is they are unaware of the frustration!

Example

"Let's spoon tonight," says the wife. The husband took her request of affection to mean something more, possibly an invitation to have sex. This is not sex... this is the component that the wife is attempting to use to distinguish a form of affection that can nurture a more passionate connection.

Most couples enjoy being touched in the beginning stages of their relationship. You can probably remember a time when you and your partner could not keep your hands off each other. But you do need to keep in mind how to sustain affection within the marriage to keep the excitement of passion going. You might notice that over time the affection fades and the opportunities to connect are far and few between.

So often, couples may refer to the term "affection" or "showing affection" in a purely physical context. Affection is not solely based on touching one another or a sexual relationship. In fact, that is a very narrow lens and somewhat limiting. There are several types or ways of showing affection. In this section of the book, we are going to focus on distinguishing three paradigms that affection can unhealthily displace and damage your relationship.

1. Affection should always lead to sexual intercourse.

If this is your belief, we want you to pause, because it is vital to understand that being affectionate can, in fact, increase or lead to having sexual intercourse; however, it doesn't **always** have to. When your partner feels as though their affection **always** has to lead to a sexual obligation, it can potentially impact their ability to feel secure within the relationship. In other words, snuggling, caressing and hugging are all important on their own and also involves a degree of vulnerability that can make you feel comfortable or uncomfortable if there is the silent rule in the relationship that affection translates to having sexual intercourse. *If this continues to happen within the* *relationship, the desire to show affection lessens, the sex lessens and all forms of affection cease.*

Example

A married couple came in for counseling, struggling with affection in their marriage. The wife said she didn't trust her husband's affection any longer because he always wants and expects her to have sex from any little form of affection. The husband said, "Well yeah, is that unreasonable to want sex if my wife is being affectionate with me?" During the sessions we discussed both of their concerns and methods to understand each other's ways of being affectionate. In fact, the couple was able to build a good connection, which avoided sending and receiving the wrong message.

2. Affection - Rejecting

Couples displaying rejecting behaviors towards their partner will often exhibit certain behaviors consciously or unconsciously: dismissive, shutdown, be standoffish, isolate or give the cold-shoulder. These behaviors can damage a relationship. They can trigger a sense of doubt, fear mistrust, shame, uncertainty that you are good enough, or overall rejected. When this happens it simply means you are unable to communicate what and how you feel in the moment. Instead, you reject your partner's attempts to show affection, leaving them hurting because of the lack of communication and connection, which can last for minutes, hours or days, depending on the severity.

Think about it, you can be sitting two feet away from the person you love and feel like you are two miles away - arms crossed, on the phone, back turned, unconcerned about your pain, and overall disinterested in you. Then after a while, both parties begin playing the dangerous rejection game, which creates a major wall, causing the relationship to starve from lack of affection. The truth is affection should NEVER be used as a rejection weapon.

3. Affection as a Control Tactic

Couples have ways of getting their partners to do what they want. We can be indirect by displaying a sense of giving or not receiving affection, depending on the circumstances, as a method of control to get our way or what we want. Believe it or not, this is fairly common in relationships.

Example

A husband could attempt to withhold affection until his wife agrees with him to watch what he wants on television, or the wife woman may give affection to get her husband to finally fix something around the house.

Using affection as a control tactic is never associated with happy relationships. Those who perceive that their partner's attempt to control them tend to be less satisfied with their relationships and are less secure or feel resentful toward their partner. In other words, when a partner feels that his/her partner is trying to pressure them into behaving a certain way and that need isn't met, it can actually *hinder* the relationship from growing. As a result, they feel unloved and unaccepting of your future attempts of affection. Overall, the results suggest that using affection unhealthily could damage your relationship in the long run, especially if your partner is convinced that your affections fall into one of the paradigms discussed in this chapter.

Learning how to give and receive affection freely to one another strengthens the overall bond. Affection, when done in a healthy way, demonstrates that you care, like and love your partner. Couples must consider their roles and motives when showing affection to each other. Use affection to grow your connection. Have honest conversations about your roles, intentions, likes and dislikes. Take notice of where you are on within the three paradigms.

Cultivating A Healthy Sexual Relationship

Many couples feel they have no time to cultivate the sexual and/or intimate parts of the relationship. A lack of physical contact can lead to a heightened sense of irritability and/or depression.

Physical intimacy when cultivated, is special because it is an act in which you are giving, enjoying and trusting each other. When physical intimacy is not cultivated, it can lead to feeling disconnected and/or dissatisfied. The relationship then is in need of reenergizing, to rejuvenating, and renewing.

Many couples struggle with the disconnection between their sexual desires and expectations of a healthy sexual life for their relationship. Every couple is different. It is important to define what a healthy sexual relationship is for your marriage – for example, frequency, likes and dislikes. Having a discussion may be totally out of the question for some couples. Oftentimes, couples do not know how to safely have a conversation about their expectations. This is where we recommend seeking counseling for an impartial view.

Many couples choose to settle for a sexless marriage - basically, they become roommates, because the partner with the higher sex drive is often left feeling neglected or undesired, while the partner with the lower sex drive often feels pressured or obligated to have sex. Another reason a couple may struggle in their sex life is that they are totally unaware that their sex life is a symptom of the problem, but not actually the real problem. Both reasons are valid. However, finding a happy medium that cultivates loving affection, can get your relationship back on track sooner than later.

Below is a quick guide that will help you cultivate a sexual partnership.

1) **Be Clear About Your Wants and Needs Regarding Sex.** Yes, you may have differences and preferences. Is it that you want sex, or is it other needs that are more nonsexual affection, such as kissing, hugging, or proof of your partner's love?

2) **Negotiate a Happy Medium.** Here is where you both create a mutual agreement on the average times per week and month you will have sex. Find a happy medium of the frequency that you both can live with.

3) **Put Sex on the Calendar.** Putting sex on the calendar is vital. Some couples in the very beginning when we suggest scheduling sex, say it doesn't feel natural. Scheduling sex reassures your partner that you have them on your mind. Over time, sex in the relationship becomes normalized.

4) **Become Innovative.** This is usually the issue of doing the "same old, same old." Mix it up a little bit. Get out of the same routine. Change the scenery, wear sexy outfits, take showers together.

5) **Foreplay.** Sexual energy is built up before you even reach the bedroom or even begin touching one another. It is easier to have one orgasm and even multiple orgasms when the pot of desire has been simmering.

CHAPTER 9

DOES YOUR RELATIONSHIP LACK AFFECTION?

Normal relationships grow despite ups and downs. However, when a relationship is lacking affection, it is hard to maintain balance.

- How often do you find yourself feeling alone and longing for affection from your partner?
- How often do you wish that your partner was more affectionate?
- Maybe you have tried to express how you feel but to not avail, so you go unsatisfied regarding affection.

If any of the above sound familiar, then you are experiencing a common problem known to many couples that have been in relationship for any period of time, of which can put a real strain on the relationship. Dr. Firestone's researchers estimated that 30-60 percent of married individuals in the United States will have an affair at some point in their relationship, highlighting one of the main reasons is affection waning over time. Couples who feel that there is a lack of affection in their marriage often feel that there is something wrong with them. Being on the receiving end of the lack of affection can be hard, but it can be naturally restored.

Showing and receiving affection can help turn a negative experience into a positive experience through one simple act. However, being affectionate is a learned skill, which eventually becomes a way of being within the relationship. We look at affection as an experience or an action of being connected with one another. Being affectionate requires the couple to be willing to be open and vulnerable. However, if one or both feel as though they are unable to communicate their feelings, it can create a wedge between them. Although choosing to show affection is an asset that can bring the couple closer, at the same time, it can be frightening and can trigger some fear, which can cause distance if not addressed.

As humans, in order to cope, we create defense mechanisms to protect ourselves from being hurt. These defense mechanisms are usually formed early in life. We often respond automatically, sometimes unaware of what caused the reaction or the impact on the other person, particularly those closest to us. A lot of these emotions can be tough topics to discuss, but more than anything you want to figure out how to connect with the wonderful person you married.

Our primary focus becomes our day-to-day living, work, home, family, but we often neglect our connection to one another. We will share in the next section an exercise on how to bring that connection back with the 4-Step Affection Audit.

How to Show Affection in Your Relationship

In this section of the book, we will share the 4-Step Affection Audit. You may be asking yourself: What is the 4-Step Affection Audit? We are taught how to show and how to receive affection. In most cases, very early in the relationship we get it right. The relationship usually becomes problematic the longer you are together. We tend to not notice our partner, what is working and/or what's not working, and how can we get back on track. These are the behavioral patterns couples get stuck in that almost always drive the couple down a dysfunctional path. Couples will continue to remain in affectionless relationships until they become fully aware of themselves, and their partners receive and give affection.

Keep in mind, we all have different preferences, so you need to explore what your partner's likes and dislikes are now. You may be surprised that they have changed. Auditing the relationship from time to time helps the couple evaluate their progress and explore where improvement is needed.

Let's get started on the 4-Step Affection Audit.

- **Step 1: Awareness**
- **Step 2: Approachability**
- **Step 3: Acknowledgement**
- **Step 4: Feedback**

Step 1: Awareness

As we mentioned in the previous chapter, just because you are not an affectionate person, does not mean that you cannot try to be more affectionate towards your partner, if that is what he/she desires. However, it is not possible unless you become aware of yourself and your partner. In other words, there is an important correlation between being aware and the overall success of your relationship.

Are you aware of what you want and what your partner wants?
Do you know why you and your partner behave the way they do?
Are you aware of your day-to-day actions?

These are important questions that you will be exploring at the end of this chapter.

However, what these explanations tell us is simply that the couple is lacking awareness, which is an important aspect to have within the relationship, because it means that you have a sound understanding of who your partner is or has become. When you are aware, you are able to self-regulate, explore and effectively engage with your partner and offer the affection that is needed.

Consider this: It could be normal for us to hear various phrases such as, "*I'm just not as affectionate as you are;*" or "*I grew up in a family where we didn't hug, kiss or say I love you.*" While these are explanations as to why one does not show the affection their partner desires, they sometimes sound like excuses to the partner on the receiving end, which can often leave one partner in distress because they desire more frequent displays of affection from their partner. You must be aware of how you contribute to lack of affection in your relationship.

You both must become aware of the attitudes, behaviors and expectations that can give you the end result that you both desire in your relationship. Awareness allows you to get crystal clear with what your partner needs from you regarding affection. However, it does require you both to be willing participants.

Example

In the early years of our relationship, Greg would occasionally bring me (Cheryl) home a bar or box of milk chocolate because he knew I liked chocolate. That was early in our relationship. However, as the years went on, I grew to like dark chocolate more. While I appreciated getting the occasional chocolates, I wasn't really eating them. In fact, I was putting them on my desk to share with my co-workers. Oftentimes, I found myself not even eating any of the chocolate!

This was something that I mentioned a couple of years after doing this work. My husband's response was funny. He said, "I would have never noticed had you not told me." Now, from time to time, I get a box or bar of dark chocolates and I hardly ever share!

We decided to share this example in this section to get you thinking about how relevant it is to your relationship to be aware of your partner and how you may think you know your partner.

Step 2: Approachability

Step 2 of the Affection Audit is being approachable.

Do you feel emotionally safe with your partner?

Do you think they have a listening ear?

Do you think they are respectful of the concerns you have expressed?

Do they make you feel that your thoughts are not validated?

Do they make light of things you deem important?

Do you feel your partner has your back in good and tough times?

Here is where learning to be honest with your partner emotionally opens for both parties to become trusting in the process. If you feel like your relationship is lacking affection, asking your partners the above questions will begin to open the door of learning how to be *approachable, which essentially means to be accessible, get to know, and talk with ease.* Wouldn't it be great to be able to connect with your partner long term, where the affection flows, without feeling as though it was forced?

Answer this question: Is there something going on between you and your partner that may be getting in the way of the two of you being more affectionate? Unresolved issues can impede the process of showing each other affection in the relationship.

Example

A couple came to us for counseling. They reported their marriage was lacking physical affection. When the husband would initiate affection, the wife would unconsciously reject his affection. After the initial interview with this couple, we explored this unconscious behavior of the wife, among other issues, where she was making the husband feel like she was not approachable.

Through further exploring, they revealed that the couple had a big disagreement several months prior regarding the wife's suspicion that her husband was having an affair with a colleague he worked closely with on a project—which wasn't the case. Even though the disagreement was several months prior, the truth is, the wife was still angry and hurt about the situation, which led to her resentment. As a result, she unconsciously displayed unapproachable behaviors towards her husband.

When her husband attempted to show her physical affection, like cuddling on the sofa, holding her hand, or rubbing her back, she would decline his attempts, which left the husband feeling undesirable. In her husband's eyes, the issue was something that the wife had resolved months prior, but that was not the case.

As long as the underlying issue wasn't addressed and there were still unresolved feelings that remained, it prevented the physical affection they both desired. Don't allow personal blocks to affect the happiness of you and your partner within your marriage!

Step 3: Acknowledgment

Acknowledgment brings a solid foundation to the marriage process. In our opinion, feeling a sense of acknowledgment from your partner brings great value to the marriage. Demonstrating acknowledgment within the marriage shows that you are present in the relationship, you recognize your partner, and you are a support, even during difficult times. It takes effort and practice to do it well.

But if both partners are committed to the process, acknowledgment can be a powerful tool in your relationship.

Why is acknowledgment in a relationship so powerful?

- Acknowledgment – Can shift or lift someone's mood.
- Acknowledgment – Can lead to the couple achieving their goals.
- Acknowledgment – Can create a happier environment.
- Acknowledgment – Can build a stronger bond.
- Acknowledgment – Can increase your overall emotional well-being.
- Acknowledgment – Can cause the couple to be more conscientious.
- Acknowledgment – Can lessen stressful situations and open new avenues for more effective communication.
- Acknowledgment – Can cause a deeper understanding of one another

As humans we all want to feel like we matter. Think about it – when your partner tells you that you did a great job on the lawn, or dinner was delicious, how does that make you feel?

Do you acknowledge your partner for his/her efforts? If so, how often?

Do you feel acknowledged by your partner for your efforts?

An acknowledgment recognizes the whole of the person, both who they are being and what they are doing. An acknowledgment is more than just a statement. It focuses slightly more on who the person is being for you in the moment. There are times in every relationship where you can get stuck, unaware of damaging behaviors. Getting help with those behaviors is definitely not a bad thing.

Step 4: Feedback

Effective feedback provides the couple with a clear communication path and ends the cycle of assuming. Feedback is a valuable component of the relationship when making decisions and building a consistent, solid relationship. Most successful couples we have worked with are not only good at accepting feedback, they deliberately ask for feedback. They realize that knowing is half the battle. Feedback is a flashlight in the dark that can guide couples to the areas they are doing well and the areas where they need improvement.

Now, we want to highlight that there is a BIG difference between effective feedback and complaints. Trust us when we say that this will change your relationship for the best.

Effective Feedback - An output/result is fed-back or evaluated for the next action. It is an expression of your opinion about the product/task. Feedback comprises of both positive and negative interactions and has the scope for improvement.

Complaint – An expression of something that is unacceptable or unsatisfactory. A complaint is negative and is a statement of criticism.

Feedback is a motivational factor, whereas complaints de-motivate. There are subtle differences. For example, below are two different ways a couple could approach the same topic.

Complaint: I can't believe you didn't remember what I said! I'm never discussing anything with you again!

Effective Feedback: I really enjoy sharing my day with you. However, sometimes when you don't remember what I say, it makes me feel as though you're not listening to me. When effective feedback is present, it can potentially decrease the number of disagreements and increase the times of enjoyment. When feedback is used ineffectively, it suggests to your partner that you find something *wrong* with them, especially when you provide no effective solutions. Effective feedback can strengthen loyalty, thereby increasing value in the marriage.

Even if you are not able to meet your partner's needs at the moment, take note of how you respond. It is important to note for yourself and get clarity of how your partner has interpreted your feedback. Take note of the many factors around you before expressing your thoughts, such as your tone, your delivery, the person, and your mood.

Example

We counseled a couple named Carl and Anna. They own a diner business. The wife's job largely consisted of standing at the front desk yelling out the orders to the kitchen staff. The husband led the kitchen staff as head chef. In the beginning, the couple's roles were pretty much established. When the kitchen staff would get the order wrong, the wife would use ineffective feedback and yell at them. Anna would say, "I said hold the tomatoes on the BLT! Carl,

you need to get the kitchen staff in order. This keeps happening every day."

They were brand new kitchen staff and were being trained. The wife's feedback elicited feelings of shame from her husband and the kitchen staff because of how the feedback was delivered. In session, we worked on ways Anna could yell out the orders and give a course of action without shaming her husband or the staff. Her ineffective feedback affected their relationship in a negative way at home. The lack of affection was one of the biggest factors.

After going the through the Affection Audit, Anna changed the way she spoke to her husband and the kitchen staff, which took some time. Instead of shaming, she said exactly what was missing from the orders. Instead, Anna began to yell things like, "Sending the BLT back; it has tomatoes;" or "Sending back the BLT to remove the tomatoes." Even though she was still yelling at them when they sent up a wrong order, she no longer yelled statements about what they were doing incorrectly that could potentially shame them. Anna was giving clear, actionable, effective feedback. Carl and Anna's relationship, their business and the staff experienced a 180-degree change for the good.

Implementing Effective Feedback

When effective feedback is present, it improves and helps build trust and confidence within the couple's relationship. Remember effective feedback mechanisms that can potentially prevent complaints and cultivate a loving, transparent relationship.

The Process for Implementing Effective Feedback

The Receiver

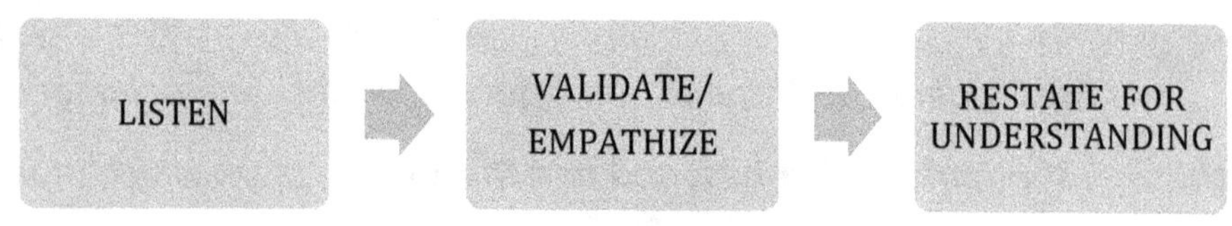

The Giver

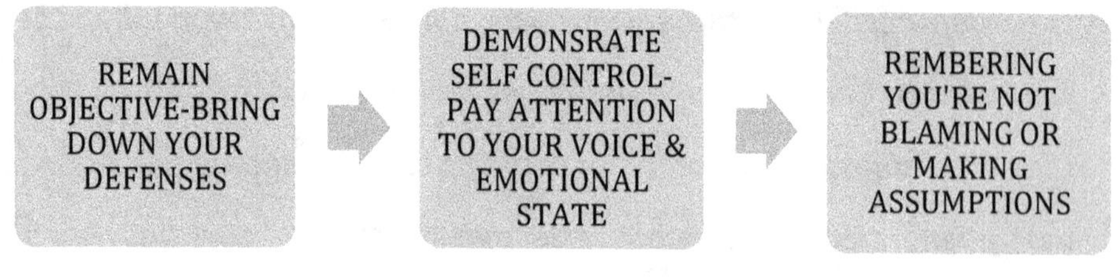

EFFECTIVE FEEDBACK TOOL CYCLE

Details of feedback Date, Time	What did I comprehend?	Am I able to deliver?	What are the opportunities present?	Immediate action taken

Part III - Chapter Highlights at A Glance:

Understanding the Importance of Affection

- Let's start with the definitions. The dictionary definition of the word "affection" is, "a gentle feeling of fondness and liking."
- When you are affectionate towards your partner they feel deeply cared for and know that you are there for them.
- When we look at affection from a biological/neuroscience research from Deepak Chopra point of view in his book The Path to Love, affection in a relationship works by rewiring the brain in a direction where love actually becomes a healing force. A simple act of affection influences your partner's hormones. It has even shown where it aids in cell repair and even homeostasis, which is biological self-regulation and self-repair.
- Theoretically, love and affection seem to go hand-in-hand.
- Affection is a powerful ACTION word. You can tell your partner you love them. However, show them your love through kisses, hugs, rubs, I love you texts and calls.
- Affection is a vital ingredient in your relationship. When one partner is affectionate toward the other, the following messages are sent: *"You are important to me." "I will care for*

you and protect you." "I am concerned about the problems you face and will be there for you when you need me."

Distinguishing Healthy Affection in the Marriage

- Affection is normal and is another essential "A" that a marriage needs to be successful.
- Oftentimes, it can be hard to distinguish between affection, intimacy and sex and other related things. So, now that you know what affection is, you should also know what it's not.
- Showing affection to your partner feeds the overall wellness of the mind, body and soul of the relationship. It's rarely impossible to maintain a healthy relationship with displays of affection over the years.
- Your marriage requires affection, such as physical touch and verbal gestures from each other. However, it's important to understand how each of you receives and gives affection. It provides for a better understanding of how to convey affection in your relationships.
- Three paradigms that affection can unhealthily displace that can damage your relationship.

  1) When your partner feels that their affection must **always** lead to a sexual obligation, it can potentially impact their ability to feel secure within the relationship.

2) Couples who display rejecting behaviors toward their partners will often consciously or unconsciously, through negative behaviors, dismiss, shutdown, be standoffish, isolate, or give the cold-shoulder. These behaviors can damage a relationship.

3) Attempting to use affection as a controlling tactic is generally not a strategy associated with happy relationships.

Identifying If Your Relationship Is Lacking Affection

- Dr. Firestone's researchers estimated that 30-60 percent of married individuals in the United States will have an affair at some point in their relationship, highlighting one of the main causes is affections waning over time.
- The 4-Step Affection Audit - **Awareness**, **Approachable, Acknowledgment, Effective Feedback**

  Step 1: Awareness - When you are aware, you are able to self-regulate, explore, and effectively engage with your partner with the amount of affection needed.

  Step 2: Approachable - Learning how to be approachable, which essentially means to be accessible, get to know, and talk with ease.

  Step 3: Acknowledgment - Demonstrating acknowledgment of one another shows that you are present in the relationship, you recognize your partner and you are a support even during difficult times.

Step 4: Effective Feedback- When effective feedback is present, it can potentially decrease the number of disagreements and increase more times of enjoyment.

CHAPTER TAKEAWAY

If your marriage is lacking affection, it is important to address it sooner than later. You can learn how to protect and nurture your marriage. This also decreases the chances of outside sources hurting the marriage or gradually drifting apart, and it creates the opportunity to have a successful, long-term, flourishing relationship. If you want to protect your marriage, it is important that you consider implementing displays of affection to your partner that makes them happy.

Part IV: The Agreement

"We have the greatest prenuptial agreement in the world. It's called love."

~ Gene Perret

Chapter 10

WHAT IS A COUPLE'S AGREEMENT?

In our experience, most couples are not familiar with a Couple's Agreement. In plain English, a Couple's Agreement is a document created by the couple. It is not a legally binding contract.

A Couple's Agreement is an understanding that you have with your partner that can bulletproof your relationship. We had a big "A-ha!" moment with this approach upon suggesting to couples they begin practicing new habits within their relationship. The ideas shared here are very structured, combining verbal and written practices to help couples achieve very specific results. We have found that with practice, time and the days of work invested, the practice is a present to your life individually and as a couple.

The agreement works by exploring what the relationship means to both the individual and the collective couple. This includes the essential components to "us." By learning to shift your perspective from I-focused to we-focused, you become more present to the needs of your partner and to those whom you are called to serve in life and in the marketplace.

What do you want in your marriage? Really give this question some thought? It is imperative to be totally clear with one another. Here's an example of why. A married couple came to counseling and we had them clarify what their marriage looks like now since they have been married for 15 years and their goals have evolved over time. Neither of them had verbally discussed or clarified a plan for their marriage.

As you begin to work as "we" you will become clearer on your next steps to take in achieving the ideal life you both have dreamed. Shifting from "I" did this" and "I did that;" to "we did this," and "we did that," recognizes the contributions of the whole. We can always identify a reason why the relationship isn't working. However, implementing a couple's agreement today can make the relationship better. Both parties need to know exactly what the other's expectations are in order to cultivate a successful marriage. Being clear is the only way it will happen.

Before beginning our business together, we had to consider the agreement and how to operate as a couple within the agreement without losing the sense of self. You may love each other. It became helpful to us to get total clarity. It answers some real questions and takes the guesswork out of the picture. You may not operate as effectively in acceptance, appreciation and showing affection if there is not an agreement present. The "Couple's Agreement" is undoubtedly formulated as a partnership where couples operating out of their gifts together, will begin to ignite the "Power Couple" within them both. As we always say, **when couples unite, greatness is bound to happen**!

We've learned to combine our passions and the gifts of relationship coaching, empowering couples in their relationships and businesses, and making more money than we could have ever dreamed we could make together, without sacrificing our marriage, our family or our fun! That is what we want to bring out in every couple out there.

In the previous sections of the book, we have gone through the importance of acceptance, appreciation, and affection in your relationship. Through the Couple's Agreement, all of these are mobilized in a way that benefits both of you. This is why having a Couple's Agreement can strengthen your relationship, because you know what you and your partner want from each other. No more dropping hints and hoping your partner will pick up on them.

The Couple's Agreement is not a contract. It is an agreement that sets forth a detailed understanding between married couples. The Couple's Agreement is designed to prevent future problems of misunderstanding. The Couple's Agreement is a purposeful verbal/written agreement that intentionally affirms and cultivates the mission of the marriage.

The Couple's Agreement is for couples committed to the ongoing agreement process of growing personally and collectively – where the marriage has the potential to become healthy and long-lasting. Implementing the Couple's Agreement is not primarily just about the couple. It becomes a culture shift that radiates from the core of their relationship, from which others can benefit, as well.

The original vision of your relationship may have changed without any discussion on how to cultivate the journey of marriage. In cases like this, a couple can struggle. Couples who have been married for quite some time, look back over the years they have invested time to develop a clear, intentional Couple's Agreement that uncovers hidden opportunities, opportunities that ensure the couple remain in sync with one another. The Couple's Agreement must be clear to both parties. This means laying out the marital duties, the needs and actions that each party can actually follow. The contract must be clear and measurable.

Example

I am willing to be more supportive. I will not work, but I am willing to ask you twice a day if I can help you with anything.

Who is the Contract Between?

The Couple's Agreement is exactly what it sounds like. Partners literally negotiate for what they need from each other and what they are willing to do for each other. This can almost *never* be done without a counselor, coach or other skilled third party, because in spite of its potential, it is a disaster waiting to happen. The skilled third party is neutral and will keep the couple on track and help them define their terms as clearly as possible. The Couple's Agreement is a document that is broken into three parts:

Acceptance – Appreciation – Affection

The couple will write the agreement together and each party will sign it. The agreement gives your marriage the structure for an honest conversation that you may not have had in a long time or may have never had. As a result, you and your partner will feel safer, loved, seen and heard. In this process, silent expectations are eliminated, highlighting what is really important for you individually and as a couple. If you have a wonderful marriage already, the agreement will enhance what already exists. For couples who are struggling, it will give you a structure to follow.

Why is the Couple's Agreement a Good Idea?

The Couple's Agreement is a good idea:

- Upon entering the marriage.
- When substantial conflicts cannot be resolved with simple conversation.
- To lessen stress and/or anger that may arise from ongoing conflict.
- To lessen the chances of separation.

A strong Couple's Agreement unifies expectations. This potentially has the power to radically transform a marriage by bringing more happiness and sustainability. The decision to create a Couple's Agreement moves your marriage to living with an intentional purpose. This will take both partners to create new habits of their own choosing to move in a new exciting direction. Thus, implementing the 4 A's of marriage can potentially reduce stress and foster marital bliss.

The Couple's Agreement begins to align each individual. This framework provides a stronger foundation for the marriage. It also begins to build trust within the relationship. We have found that this agreement has reduced conflicts and has brought unity to the marriage. Conflicts are no longer avoided, nor do they become increasingly and unnecessarily complex. Instead, everything unclear is addressed through workable solutions, aiding in any future concerns before things escalate and become uncontrollable. Discovering the power in the Couple's Agreement and using it will only strengthen your relationship.

A couple could create a Couple's Agreement every three, six or nine months that lays out the purpose, values, communication, and the like that each partner commits to during that period. At the end of the agreed time, the couple can choose to renew their agreement and/or adjust its terms.

SAMPLE COUPLE'S AGREEMENT

Starting this process out right is important. Preparation time is key. Successful marriages do not just happen. Both parties must commit to the process and implementing the techniques. First, start by reading the book and doing the exercises. Before we start this process we always pray together and ask God to guide our hearts and spirit.

Do not rush this process or remind your partner of all the things you think they need to change. The goal of the Couple's Agreement is for both parties to focus on the overall success of the marriage, where the only person you have the power to change is you. When you commit to being more accepting of who you genuinely are, it will not only transform your marriage but your entire life. Trust the process.

Create meaningful results in your marriage. Knowing is not enough. Applying what you have learned is a MUST! Going through ups and downs in your marriage is normal. However, learning to master being in your marriage can happen if you know what works and what does not work in your marriage.

- **1st** - Acceptance provides a deeper understanding of yourself and partner.
- **2nd** - Appreciation recognizes the necessity to appreciate one another, while highlighting the value you both bring to the unit.
- **3rd** – Affection distinguishes healthy affection in the marriage.

When creating the Couple's Agreement, it is important to be consistent. Feel free to use the exercises in the book as a guide. For each section, as you come into agreement, write it down. You will find those answers will become very helpful when you begin to craft your Couple's Agreement.

The Conclusion

"Enjoy every single moment. The good, the bad, the beautiful, the ugly, the inspiring, the not-so-glamorous moments. And thank God through it all."

~**Meghan Matt**

You Finally Did It!

All of us humans need the concepts of the 4 A's in our lives. At times it can be a struggle in the couple dynamic when we don't have the tools of *Acceptance, Appreciation, Affection* and *Agreement.* This book covered four powerful strategies for couples to explore their current relationships and how to shift problematic behaviors, habits and conditioning to create the relationship they have always dreamed.

We hope you feel more connected than ever after going through this book together. We hope that you feel more capable of understanding each other's need to communicate how you are feeling. This is exactly why the divorce rate in America is through the roof! If your car breaks down, you have one of two options - buy a new one or go have it repaired. People tend not to want to repair what is broken. They just want to replace it if they can. Repairing it requires work, time and effort. With this mindset so prevalent in our culture, we have started treating marriage in the same way.

By working hard on your marriage and trying to understand your partner's needs, you will definitely see a positive change in your relationship. We are glad you decided to take time out from your busy schedule to devote to your relationship and read this book. The material that we have provided will definitely help you in building a stronger marriage. Feel free to re-read this book and do the exercises within the workbook so you can continue to create the best relationship possible. In the workbook, we have included exercises that can help you and your partner work towards creating a relationship that is fully capable of meeting both of your needs through the application of strategies you've learned in this book.

With the help of these strategies, you will have successfully prepared yourself to take the steps to create the best possible relationship. Together, you will continue to take the steps to reach your common goals for your marriage and understand the importance of *acceptance, appreciation, affection*, and a *relationship agreement* in your marriage.

You are learning to take risks and getting closer to your dreams, despite the obstacles in your path. You are learning to be vulnerable with each other and connect on an emotional, physical, and mental level.

We are thrilled that you chose to include us in your journey to building a better marriage and a healthier relationship. We want nothing but the best for you. We hope that your relationship thrives after applying the concepts in this book to your love life.

When Couples Unite, Greatness is Bound to Happen!

REFERENCES

Berger, E. M. (1952). The relation between expressed acceptance of self and expressed acceptance of others. *Journal of Abnormal & Social Psychology, 47,* 778-782.

Chopra, Deepak. *The Path to Love: Spiritual Strategies for Healing*. Three Rivers Press, 2006.

Firestone, Robert W., et al. *Sex and Love in Intimate Relationships*. American Psychological Association, 2008.

Goldsmith, Dr. Barton "Independence and Interdependence-What's Best for Love?" *Psychology Today*, Sussex Publishers, www.psychologytoday.com/us/blog/emotional-fitness/201307/independence-and-interdependence-whats-best-love.

"Healthy Dependency vs. Codependency." *Live Well with Sharon Martin*, 5 Nov. 2020, www.livewellwithsharonmartin.com/healthy-dependency-vs-codependency/.

Personal Relationships, vol. 22, no. 1, 2015, pp. 536–549., doi:10.1111/pere.2015.22.issue-1.

Rand, Kevin & Cheavens, Jennifer. (2012). Hope Theory. The Oxford Handbook of Positive Psychology, (2 Ed.). 10.1093/oxfordhb/9780195187243.013.0030.

Sean M. Horan & Melanie Booth-Butterfield (2010) Investing in Affection: An Investigation of Affection Exchange Theory and Relational Qualities, Communication Quarterly, 58:4, 394-413, DOI: 10.1080/01463373.2010.524876

Srini Pillay, MD. "Greater Self-Acceptance Improves Emotional Well-Being." *Harvard Health,* 16 May 2016, www.health.harvard.edu/blog/greater-self-acceptance-improves-emotional-well-201605169546.

APPENDIX

Acceptance and Arguments

Does accepting your partner mean you won't ever argue again? A healthy type of arguing is good for any relationship. In fact, we argue; however, it's a healthy disagreement.

Cheryl's Side

The other day, I was talking to Greg about something that happened to me during the course of my day, and while I was in the middle of the story, he asked me about something on a completely different topic. To me, it felt like he was not present in the conversation and I didn't feel validated. This would happen again if I did not communicate to my husband that I was bothered by this. Greg would never have known that something was wrong. While telling my story, I felt as if he was not hearing me. I was able to communicate to Greg immediately how I felt about what just happened.

Greg's Side

I had no idea. I took ownership right away and apologized for interjecting. But the thing is, even though I felt like I was still listening to what my wife was saying, my actions caused her to feel unheard.

Greg acknowledging how I didn't feel heard is key, not that he felt as though he was listening and agreeing, but by him also being conscious of his actions going forward stopped the miscommunication that could have caused a major divide between us in the long run as a couple.

Gaining the skills to address the miscommunication right away has aided our marriage in growing, because ultimately, you are two different individuals who have different perspectives. A healthy conflict can be beneficial for your relationship. It can even bring the two of you closer, when done correctly. Remember, couples have to be taught how to be in a marriage. It doesn't just happen!